Chuckle Giggle Laugh

by
Jaspreet Gill

Chuckle Giggle Laugh

(A CosmoDigital Publication)

Copyright © Jaspreet Gill

Disclaimer
Events and conversations in this book have been re-written from author's memories of real conversations. But the names and characteristics used in content are ficticious to avoid identification with any person, place or event directly or indirectly. Such identification or resemblance if any is co-incidental and unintentional.

Give feedback on the book at:
publications@cosmodigital.com

Preface

Every parent and teacher knows that young growing up children can be very funny and entertaining. Their interaction with their parents, teachers or other kids in class or otherwise sometimes lead to funny conversations. While at school or outside at play their conversations are truely funny and remarkable. Most parents and teachers would share and enjoy these funny moments.

Being a teacher and a parent I have been keeping mental note of such conversations since many years. These fun filled conversations have been re-written from my memories of them using fictional names and compiled into this book for your pleasure. Hope you will enjoy !

ILLUSTRATIONS

JASPREET GILL & HARKIRAT GILL

AM I SUPPOSED TO HAVE MORE FEET?

Before the lunchtime, the teacher told the kids to get ready to go outside, to play for a while. The children started to change into their outside shoes. The teacher noticed that Jack was wearing the shoes the other way and she pointed it out.

Teacher: O Oh, Jack, your shoes are on the wrong feet.

Jack: But Ms. Jen, these are the only feet I have.

THIS IS TOUGH!

Sam is a 4 and a half year old boy. It was math time. The teacher gave him numbers to do addition. It was his first time adding the bigger numbers.

Teacher: Okay Sam, tell me what is 7+8?

Sam: (after struggling to count on his fingers) I can't tell. I don't have enough fingers! I need more fingers to count this one.

ALL ABOUT WHALES...

Teacher: (writing on the board) ... Whales ... are mammals!
Billy: If you take away the 'l' and 's', it makes 'Mamma'.
Nathan: So if we and whales are mammals, that means they are our cousins.
Billy: And what do whales eat?
Nathan: I think Chickens, like us. Remember, our cousins!

Billy: Okay tell me, what are the babies of whales called?
Nathan: Cows.
Billy: No, calves.
Nathan: Close enough!

YOU WANT A MEAN AUNT?

Molly, a kindergartener, was back from her trip to Disney. One morning she was talking to the teacher about her trip.
Molly: You know, I found my uncle a wife at Disney.
Teacher: Really! Where?
Molly: At Disney. She is Cinderella's step sister.
Then Molly went closer to the teacher and whispered in her ear, "You know why? Because her step sisters were mean. Then my uncle will have a Meany wife."

WHY CAN'T I DO THAT?

The kindergartners were learning about the Presidents of America. Jack made a beard and a mustache on Mr. Kennedy's picture. The teacher asked why he did it.

Jack: Well, most of the Presidents had a beard and a mustache, so I thought to do that. And I think Mr. Kennedy looks good with that.

MISSING TEETH MYSTERY!

The kindergartners are always interested in knowing everything about the Presidents of USA. The teacher was talking about George Washington.

Teacher: George Washington lost all his teeth when he was the President.
John: May be he was eating a lot of candy. So what did he eat without his teeth?
Jackie: I think he ate Gerber apple sauce. My baby brother eats that, he also has no teeth.

You too! Huh!

NOBODY UNDERSTANDS ME
Teacher: (to innocent 3 year old) Hey Olivia, How are you?

Olivia: I am three.

Teacher: No, How "ARE" you?

Olivia: I already said three.

STAY FIT.
Teacher: Do you know James Madison was the shortest President.

Jack: Not any more.

Teacher: Why?

Jack: Because he's dead.

Another Kid from back: Why was he the shortest?

Jack: May be he never went to YMCA for exercise.

WHO'S CUTE?
One morning Nicholas was dropped off by his mom and his little baby brother.

Teacher to Nicholas: Hey Nicholas, your brother is so cute.

Nicholas: Yeah, but I am cuter.

MOLLY MAIDS!

Ms. Jamie told Peter and Sam to clean up their messy art table. She gave a wet towel to each of them.

Peter (to Sam while cleaning): Hey, we are the cleaning ladies.
Sam: No silly, we are the cleaning men.
Peter: How can we be men, we are still boys.
Sam: Don't worry, it is just an imagination.

THESE KIDS ARE SMART

One afternoon during lunch time, I was sitting with Brianna, Anna and Jack (all around the age of 5).

Anna: So how do we get our last names?
Brianna: Depends on who you marry.
Teacher (kidding): Yes, for example if you marry Willy Wonka, you will be called Mrs.Wonka.
Brianna: Oh that sounds weird. I will marry someone with the last name as Mr. Sippi.
Jack: Why?
Brianna: Because then I will be called Mrs.Sippi (Mississippi), get it...?

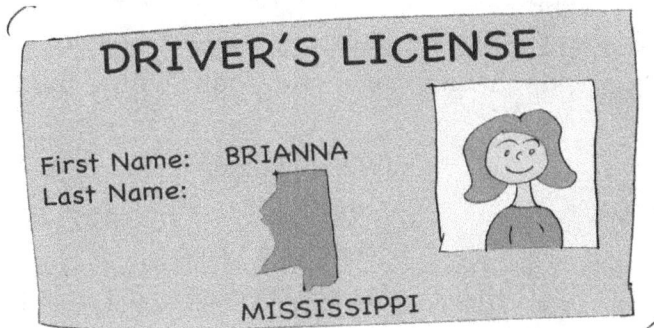

DRIVER'S LICENSE

First Name: BRIANNA
Last Name:

MISSISSIPPI

LET ME FINISH

Ms. Kate and 5 year old Peter was working on the same table doing some craft work. She saw a band-aid on his arm. Ms. Kate asked Peter what had happened.

Peter: I told my mom...

Before Peter could finish, Ms. Kate interrupted.

Ms. Kate: Peter, You don't tell your mom, you always ask her, okay.

Peter: Okay, I asked my mom I got hurt!

24/7 AVAILABLE!

The kindergartners were working on their binders about the American Presidents.

Sam: (very tired) Ms. Susan, why do we have to write and remember so much about the Presidents? We can find everything on Google, right?

NOT MY FOOD

The kindergartners were working on the Food Pyramid poster. They were supposed to sort the food pictures and then glue them to the particular category they belonged. Max was hesitating to put the picture of meat balls on the Food pyramid.

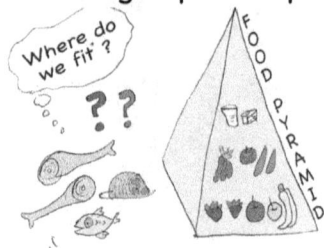

Max: I can't paste the meat picture?

Teacher: Why?

Max: Because I am a vegetarian!

OLIVIA? PET?

We were all talking about our pets. Now it was John's turn to talk about it.

Teacher: So John, do you have any pets?
John: No, but we have Olivia, my sister.

MY SISTER

MAGIC PENCIL

Sam was sitting idle and not doing any work. It was almost lunch time and the teacher wanted him to finish fast. But Sam was not in the mood to be done.

Teacher: Sam, finish your work please.
Sam: But I already did it.
Teacher: Where? I don't see it.
Sam: That's because I did it with my invisible pencil.

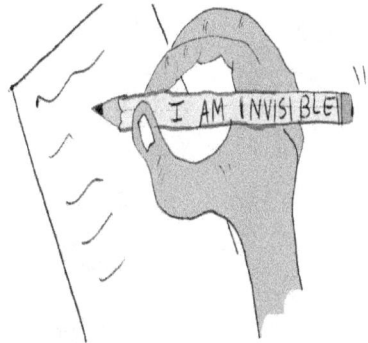

I AM INVISIBLE

SO WHO IS IN THE ZOO?

Emery and Charlie were playing with the farm animals.

Emery: Why did you put hippo in the farm house?
Charlie: Because he's been kicked out of the zoo.

ARE YOU SURE, OLIVIA?

Sarah and John were eating snack when Olivia's mom and dad came to drop her. After they left, Olivia went to the snack table and started eating with them.
... After a while,

John: Olivia, your mom and dad look the same. Are they twins?
Olivia: I think so.

THAT WE'LL HAVE TO CHECK

Billy and Sam were arguing about something that I heard for the first time. I am guessing most of us have not heard about this very interesting fact about an Octopus.

Billy: Do all the animals poop?
Sam: Yes.
Billy: No, Octopus doesn't.
Sam: Yes, it does.
Billy: No, it doesn't. I have never seen one doing it.

I AM BETTER

One time the teacher found a writing paper, without a name.
Teacher: I have found a lost paper without a name. John, is this your handwriting?
John: No, mine is better.

YUMMY BUGS!

While the children were playing outside, Peter and Emery were talking about the carnivores, herbivores and insectivores.

Peter: My sister was an insectivore when she was 2.

Emery: Why?

Peter: She used to eat bugs.

MAMA MIA

It was snack time; Peter and John were sitting together and talking about sleepover.

Peter: Are you coming to my house for sleepover?

John: No, I can't. Over the weekend I sleep with my mom.

Peter: I sleep with my mom whenever my dad is away.

John: Who sleeps with her otherwise?

Peter: My dad.

John: Why?

Peter: Because their beds are connected, ...I think.

CONFUSION

Emma was not eating her lunch. The teacher noticed and she came to her.

Teacher: Hey Emma, you are not eating? Are you full?

Emma: No, I am four.

WHO CAME FIRST?

Billy was kind of day dreaming one day. Suddenly he said to his friend, "Are all the teachers born before the children?"

SWEET SUSAN

Three year old Susan was playing outside. It was hot that day. She was sweating. She went to the teacher and wanted to tell her how sweaty she was.

Susan: Ms. Jamie, there is a lot of juice coming from my body.

DUDE, YOU JUST TOLD ME!

There was a new boy, Bobby, in the class since two weeks only.

He was working with Red Rods (Montessori work).Suddenly he started jumping around them.

Peter: Hey Roby, stop jumping.

Bobby: I am Bobby, not Roby.

Peter: Okay Bobby, stop jumping.

Bobby: Hey, how do you know my name?

DR. NAUGHTY

Jack and Olivia both 5 year old, were talking about what they want to be when they grow up.

Olivia: I want to be a mom.

Jack: I want to be a doctor, so that I can poke needles in people's body. That's fun!

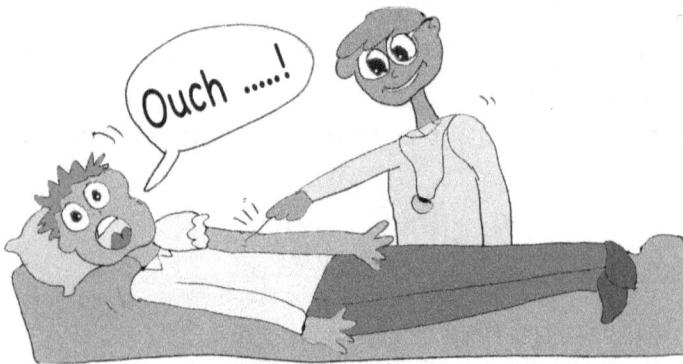

DON'T WORRY, MICHAEL

Michael, 4 year old, was all dressed up for the picture day.

Teacher: Wow Michael, you are looking very handsome today. Are you getting married? (Teasing him)

Michael: No, my mom said I can never marry.

My Dream Wedding

THAT'S OKAY, FRENCH BOY

Ms. Susan was showing the children some things that begin with the letter 'M'.

Ms. Susan: This is a pair of "Mittens". I got these when I had been to Canada. This is a "Map" of Canada. This is a picture of my "Mom", who lives in Canada. This is a "Monkey" toy, I bought this from Chicago. I also have this small version of a "Mop".

Ms. Susan: (showing a "Measuring tape"): Alright boys and girls, who can tell me what this is?

Marc: (making a sad face and so fed up with the word "Canada") I don't know. I am from France.

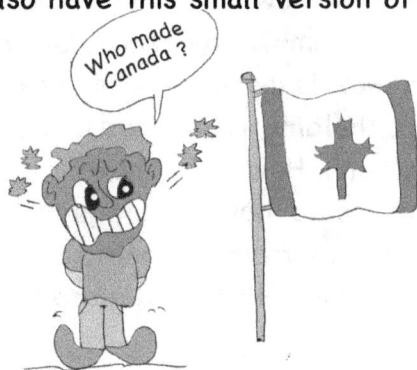

Who made Canada ?

IRISH BOY

The kindergartners were on a field trip to the Arboretum. They were divided into small groups with an adult. The teacher saw a boy and a girl running in front of everybody. She asked them where they were going.

I would love to be a chaperone !

Boy: We lost our Leprechaun.
Teacher: Leprechaun? Don't you mean Chaperone?
Boy: Oh yes, that.

OH PLEASE, LET ME GO FOR NOW

Five year old Max, was going to the bathroom. I didn't realize that he was in a hurry. I stopped him and started asking about his mom who was not feeling well few days back.
Me: Max, how is mommy doing?
Max: Ummh..... What did you say?
Me: How is mommy feeling now, she hurt her back, right?
Max (holding really bad): Emmh... my mommy?
Me: Yeah, How is she now?
Max (could hold no longer): Unnhh.....Can I tell you when I come back from the bathroom.
Poor thing! He had to go so bad.

TOO MUCH KNOWLEDGE IS A DANGEROUS THING

Molly and Peter were learning more and more about the weekdays.

Molly: I know the names of all the weekdays and also my mom told me that Monday is a week-end.

Peter: No, Monday is a week (weak) day.

Molly: So is Tuesday going to be a strong day?

GROSS... BUT NOT FOR KIDS

The kindergartners were doing their language work. The teacher had given them some words. The children were supposed to make sentences with them.

Teacher: Make a sentence with "nose".

Sarah: I saw a nose.

Teacher: That is a very short sentence. Sarah, you are a kindergartner, I expect you to make a longer sentence.

Sarah: Okay," I saw a nose full of boogers".

LISTEN CAREFULLY, MOLLY

Molly noticed that the lights were off.

Molly: Why are the lights off?

Teacher: Because we have enough light from the Sun during the day.

Molly: We don't have electricity?

Teacher: We do have electricity. But the Sun is enough to give us light right now.

Molly: Oh Okay, but why are the lights off then?v

DUNKIN DADDY

Peter to Ms. Kate:," Ms. Kate, your coffee smells like my dad."

PLEASE DON'T TELL THE PRESIDENT!
Emma and Joe were talking about their favorite TV shows.

Emma: I am going to watch SpongeBob today when I go home.
Joe: But Obama says no watching TV on week days.
Emma: Who is Obama?
Joe: I don't know. My mom just told me this.

CHECK THE YELLOW BOOK

Teacher: Alright, today we are going to talk about George Washington 1731 – 1799.
Sam: Is that his phone number?

SCARY RED
Marc and Molly were coloring on the art table.
Marc: I never color with the red marker.
Molly: Why?
Marc: Because if it gets on my shirt, it looks like blood. And that scares my mom.

A

VERY HOT SUN

Sam: Why are you coloring the Sun red?
Peter: Because my Sun is on fire.

THROW UP CONTEST WINNER!

Now this is a very interesting argument between Brendan and Emma.
Brendan: My sister threw up this morning.
Emma: My brother threw up too.
Brendan: Really! What time?
Emma: I guess 8' 0 clock.
Brendan: I think my sister threw up before 8.
Emma: So what time?
Brendan: I think 7'0 clock.
Emma: She can't. That is too early to throw up. I think my brother did it before your sister.
Brendan: No, he didn't.
Emma: Yes, he did.
Brendan: No.
Emma: Yes.

...And this yes and no went for a while.

MY NAME IS NOT ON MY SHIRT

It was St. Patrick's Day. Some kids were wearing green and also had something written on their shirts.
Brendan had "I am Irish" written on his shirt.

Teacher: Are you Irish?
Brendan: No, I am Brendan.

DON'T BREAK MY HEART

The teachers and the children went to watch a play in the auditorium. It was about "The very hungry caterpillar". The background throughout the play was a blackout. The children could see only the beautiful, colorful, shining things in the front. The caterpillar and all the food that it was eating, was all shining with LED lights. Children were amazed to see all the things moving on the stage. After the show, Molly, Peter and Emma were talking about it.

Molly: Wow! It was so beautiful, how did they even do that?
Emma: They did not do anything. I think it was all magic!
Peter: Oh no, you girls know nothing. It was no magic, it was all electrical.

A VALENTINE FOR AN INCHWORM

Sam was making his Valentine card. The teacher had told them that they were all making an Inchworm on the card and then they were supposed to write "You inched your way into my heart."

Sam to Molly: What are you writing on the card?
Molly: I am writing "I love my mom and dad".
Sam got very confused between those two sentences, started to think what to write.

Finally he wrote something and gave the card to his teacher. The teacher opened the card. Sam had written "I love you Inchworm".

YOURS TOOTH FULLY

Children are often seen discussing that who got the most money, when they lose their teeth.

Brendan: My dad said that he will give me $10,000, if I lose all my teeth at the same time.

BEWARE MOMS ...YOUR SECRETS ARE OUT!

During lunch time, Ms. Jamie and Matt were sitting on the same table.

Hope Nobody Sees me !

FROZEN FOOD

Ms. Jamie: Uhmm... Matt, your lunch smells yummy. Did mommy make it?
Matt: Yeah, she did.
Ms. Jamie: So she cooks yummy food every day.
Matt: Yes, but first she has to get it from the frozen section.

WHY WASTE TIME?

The teacher was explaining words with the **silent** letter 'K'.
Teacher (writing on the board): Our next word is "Knife". But the K is silent here.
Jack: Then why even write it, if we are not using it.

ANNE, SMARTY PANTS

Two kindergartners, Sarah and Anne were arguing about their reading level.

Sarah: I can read 2nd grade level.
Anne: I can read 8th grade level.
Sarah: No, you can't.
Anne: Yes, I can. I can do it right now. It's in my bag.
Sarah: Okay, show it.
Anne went to get the book from her bag. She came back with a book that belonged to her brother, who is in 8th grade.
Anne: See, it says on the top "8th grade level". I told you I could read.

THAT'S THE BRAND NAME, SILLY

During lunch time, Molly found a Corelle bowl on her table. She picked the bowl and started walking around the class.

Teacher: Hey Molly, why are you walking with that bowl? Whose is it?

Molly: Well, I don't know. Let me check the name under. It says C...O...R...E...L...L...E...(cor....elll...eey).

(Molly Loudly) Well, who is Corelley in our class ?

SORRY GRANDPA

Sometimes kids come up with really surprising stories or sentences. I have often wondered where they get these things from.

Jack was doing his sentences. The teacher gave them the word "grandpa".

Jack wrote down, "My grandpa is soon going to die."

Teacher (after reading the sentence): Oh my goodness, what happened to him? Is he sick?

Jack: Oh no, not that. It's that he's 65 and I think that's enough for him.

JUST DON'T FORGET "LE"

The French teacher in our school was teaching children about the names of the colors in French.

Teacher: Most of the words begin with 'Le' in French. Okay let's learn about some colors. Red is Le rouge, Blue is Le bleu, White is Le blanc, Black is Le noir, Green is Le vert. (After going through these words for a while and repeating them. The teacher started asking the children, hoping they remembered)

Teacher: Sam, what do you call white in French?

Sam (thinking for a while): Le white.

WHAT DOES DRILL MEAN?

We do fire drill in our school every year. Today was the day. After the alarm went off, the kids started lining up and we all started to move out of the classroom. But Little Max would not move.

Teacher: Come on guys, walk fast, we have to move out.

Max: But I don't see any fire. Where is the fire? Show me the fire first.

ANYTHING CAN GET TIRED

Ms. Kate: Excuse me Molly, why are you not working? You just wrote three words. You have 5 sentences to finish.

Molly: Yeah I know, but it's not my fault. It's just my pencil is really tired.

CHILLY BILLY

This conversation took place a day after the earthquake in Chile.

Teacher: So did you hear about the earthquake in Chile.

Billy: Yeah, I had been to Chile.

Teacher: Really, Wow. When did you go?

Billy: Last night.

Peter: How can you go yesterday? They had an earthquake.

Billy: I did. I also ate some food with my dad.

For a while this argument went on between Peter and Billy. But in the end we found out that Billy did go for dinner, but not Chile, he went to Red Chillies restaurant.

THAT WAS EASY

Teacher: What is meat?

Kid: Dead animal.

NO MORE BARBERS FOR DAD

That morning when Jack stepped in the classroom, he looked different. The teacher came closer to Jack.

Teacher: Good Morning Jack. Wow! You got a haircut.
Jack: Yeah, I went with my dad.
Teacher: So dad got one too.
Jack: No, he doesn't need one. He is growing old and his hair has stopped growing. No more haircuts for him.

TIT FOR TAT

One day I was at the public library and Susan from our school also came there with her mom. I saw her and she waved at me.

Me: Hi Ashley! (I was pretending that I don't know who she was)
Susan got that fast and she replied back as fast she could and said: Hi, Ms. Karen!
Ms. Karen is not my name. But Susan got the joke real fast and answered me in the same way, how I was kidding. Susan is only 4 years old.
Never think less about the thinking power of these young children. They are smarter than us.

NO, DON'T DO THAT

After the fire drill that day, Ms. Jen was asking children some questions.

Ms. Jen: So what do we do if there is a fire.
Brendan: Jump out of the window?

THAT DOES SOUND EASY...

Matt was working on his President binder.

Teacher: Good job Matt, you are doing great work. So do you want to be a President when you grow up?

Matt: No, I don't want to, because then I'll have to be mean.

Teacher: So what do you want to be?

Matt: I want to be a lawyer, it is easy. All you have to do is blah, blah, blah ....

EVERYTHING GOES TO HEAVEN

Molly and Emma were looking at the fish tank.

Molly: Yesterday, one of the fishes died.

Emma: Oh No! So where do fishes go when they die?

Molly: Fish Heaven, I think.

ACTUALLY IT'S BOTH

The teacher was working with the kindergartners.

Teacher: So boys and girls, each of you have to work hard. You all have to 'excel' to go to 1st grade.

Sam: But I thought that we have to' graduate' to go to 1st grade.

TOO MUCH KNOWLEDGE IS A DANGEROUS THING

Sam and Peter were having milk during their lunch time.

Sam: Where do we get milk from?
Peter: Cows. Don't you know that?
Sam: And where do we get the chocolate milk from?
Peter: From the Brown cows.

You better eat more....Mr.

We had a new boy, Andy in our class. He was 4 years old, and he was really thin.

Teacher: Wow Andy, you are so cute. You are such a peanut.
Peter: Well if he is a peanut, isn't the squirrel going to eat him.

REMIX

One day the teacher was talking about different countries and their languages.

Teacher: The people in England speak English, in Ireland they speak Irish, and in Spain they speak Spanish.

And so on the teacher talked about a lot other countries and the languages. The next day when the kids came back to school, the teacher thought of taking a small test.

Teacher: So who can tell me what language do they speak in Russia?

What? I thought I was a Vegetable !

Billy: I know.

Teacher: Okay Billy, what is it?

Billy: Radish.

OH DEAR!

Olivia (5year old): I lost my tooth yesterday and I got a dollar from the tooth fairy.

Molly: But last time when you lost your tooth you said you got $ 5.

Olivia: Yeah I asked my mom about it. She said something about bad economy. I didn't understand much.

WHY JAPAN?

Every Tuesday Peter used to be little worried. I found out that he didn't like going for his Piano classes each Tuesday, after school. He was eating his snack and I asked him how he was doing regarding his piano class.

Peter: I want to send my piano to the Japanese museum.

Teacher: Why?

Peter: ...I don't like it but my mom wants me to learn it.

WELL, YOU SAID IT....SO YOU DO IT!

Teacher (after checking Max's work): Oh no, I'll have to fix your handwriting. Not so good.

Max: Okay, here fix it.
Max started walking away.
Teacher: Where are you going?
Max: To do some work.
Max: But first you have to fix this work.
Max: But you said that you are going to fix it. You don't need me. Do you?

ABSTRACT ART IS EASY

Max: It is so easy to draw shapeless people.
Peter: Why?
Max: Because then you don't have to make a shape. You can just draw as you want to.

Me   Mom   Dad

WAIT TILL YOU GET MARRIED

Sam: Jack, do you know that when they get married, all mommies kiss daddies.
Jack: Ewww......gross!

SCARY LAUNDRY

In our school every Friday the classroom laundry for that week is taken by one of the family to wash and then they bring back the clean, ironed laundry back to school on Monday. So one Monday when Max came back with the laundry, this was a funny conversation.

Teacher: Thank you Max for bringing the laundry back. So who did the laundry?
Max: Me and my dad.
Teacher: What about mom?
Max: She was hiding in the closet.
Teacher: What? Why?
Max: Oh she got scared of the laundry. Then she was hiding until we finished.

IS PINK ONLY FOR GIRLS?

Emma and Peter were coloring on the same table with the teacher.
Emma: I like pink.
Teacher: I also liked pink when I was a baby.
Peter: I also liked pink when I was a baby too.
Emma to Peter: What! What! So you were a girl when you were a baby.

THIS SHOULD BE VERIFIED!

The kindergartners were reading about the American Presidents.

Teacher: So you see, they didn't had bathrooms in the White House until the 3rd President moved in.
Kid: So where did they go?
Teacher: I don't know, maybe they had an outhouse, or mobile bathrooms or a box? Well I really can't say?
All the kids: Ewe! Ewe! Ewe!

YEAH THAT'S ABSOLUTELY TRUE!

Molly and Emery were talking about their grandmas.
Molly: My grandma was a girl once.
Emery: Mine too.
Molly: Really! Well, I think all grandmas were girls.

Yeah! Those were the days!

THEY SOUND THE SAME!

Jack: Yesterday, I went to paper clips to get a haircut.
Teacher: Don't you mean Great Clips?
Jack: oh yeah, that!

MAKE RULES FOR BEES

Olivia was telling Max about her bee sting. It had happened a day before.

Olivia: They keep stinging the person, as if they are in war with the person.

Max: Yeah! And also the bees can do anything they want to because they don't have a teacher to stop them.

I am the teacher, now!

No Kidding!

WHY CAN'T I BE?

The kids were playing outside. The teachers were out watching them. It was very, very windy that day. Ms. Jen has short hair, so because of the wind it got all messed up. After a while when everyone came inside, Ms. Jen started to brush her hair. Olivia was watching her do that and this is what she said,

I am going to brush my hair all day long!

CAT
BAT
FOX

Ms. Jen

Olivia: Oh! Ms. Jen, you are such a drama queen!

THIS IS FUNNY

Brendan and Jack were sitting on the table outside, while other kids were playing. Brendan was supposed to be picked up by his grandpa that day. He was very excited about that and would not stop talking about him.

Brendan: Do you have a grandpa?

Jack: Yes, I do. Actually I have two of them.

Brendan: How old is your grandpa?

Jack: 78 years old.

Brendan: And how old is your Grandma?

Jack: 78.

Brendan: Oh! They are same age?

Jack: Yeah. That is why they married each other because they are same age.

PEELINGS OR FEELINGS!

Molly was about to start eating her lunch. She wanted to eat her orange first. But it was a whole orange and not peeled. She went to the teacher for some help.

Molly: Could you please open my orange?

Teacher: Do you mean peel it?

Molly: No, the peeling would hurt the orange, just open it.

WE CAN ALL SHARE NAMES, RIGHT?

There are always some small arguments going on in every corner of the classroom. Here is something that Emma and Brendan were arguing about.

Emma: My cat's name is Donavan.
Brendan: No, you are lying. That's my sister's teacher's name.

IS YOUR HOME A ZOO?

Emery was sitting with Sam and Molly on the art table and they were all coloring. Emery was asking both of them about their siblings.

Emery: How many kids are there in your house?
Sam: No kids, that's what my mom says.
Emery: Then who do you have?
Sam: Mom says she has monkeys.

THIS IS SO CONFUSING

Teacher: What is the baby of a horse called?
Jack: Donkey.
Teacher: No, it's a calf or a colt. Okay, what is a baby sheep called?
Jack: Oh I know that. It's a goat. Right?

50% WAS CORRECT

It is always fun to watch children learning French. One day the French teacher was teaching about the names of farm animals. After repeating some animals, she wanted to ask the children to check if they remembered.

French Teacher: What do you call 'a pig' in French?
Jerry: Le Pig.
French Teacher: No. Le Cochon.
Jerry: I was close.

FORGET THE LUNCH

Max was eating lunch at the teacher's table.

Teacher: Wow Max, your lunch looks delicious.
While the teacher was talking to Max, he was looking so deeply into her eyes. The teacher was still talking to him: So who made your lunch?
Max (still staring at her): Huh?
Teacher: Who made your lunch?
Max: Wow, look at that Ms. Kate. I am in your eyes!

You are scaring me, Max!

TOTALLY FAIR!

One day during lunch time Emery was very upset to see her lunch.
Emery: Why did mommy just give me 2 baby carrots?

Teacher: May be she just had only 2 left in the fridge.
Emery: No, I saw she had 4 left. For that I will have to check my sister's lunch. Can I? (And even before the teacher could say anything about that, Emery had already started checking her sister's lunch)
Emery: Okay, I am fine. I was right. Mom gave 2 carrots to my sister. That's okay, I'm fine.
And Emery went on with that for a while.

WOW, THIS TOOK A WHILE!

Now this was a pretty long argument with a funny ending. Two boys, Billy and Miles found an ant outside in the yard during their playtime. Billy was looking at the ant and started telling Miles about his ant story, something that happened couple days back.

Billy: One day I saw an ant and a millipede together in my yard.

Miles: So they were fighting?

Billy: The ant picked the millipede on its head.

Miles: So they were fighting?

Billy: Ant was very strong, I think.

Miles: Did the millipede bit the ant?

Billy: No.

Miles: I think millipede is stronger than the ant. It can bite.

Billy: No, but the ant was carrying it.

Miles: Isn't millipede stronger?

Billy: Yes. But the ant was carrying it, so I guess the ant is stronger.

Miles: That's not possible.

Billy: Why?

Miles: Ant can never win with millipede.

Billy: Yeah, I know.

Miles: So why are you saying that the ant is stronger and was carrying it.

Billy: Oh come on, Miles didn't I tell you already the millipede was dead and the ant was carrying it as its food.

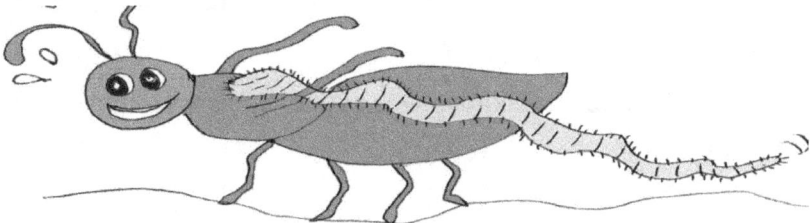

WHO PUT THAT IN THERE?

We were celebrating Chinese New Year. One of the moms had got each child a Fortune Cookie. All the children were sitting and eating snacks together. Brendan was going to try the fortune cookie for the first time. He put the cookie in his mouth. After he took a bite, he found the small paper hanging on his lips. He took it out and started telling everybody: LOOK! I FOUND MY NAME TAG IN THE COOKIE!

Think Fast

I was doing phonics with a 4 year old boy, Jim. He knew most of the letters, but when I picked the letter W, he could not sound it out. He did something very funny. While I was looking away, he flipped the letter upside down and made it look like M.

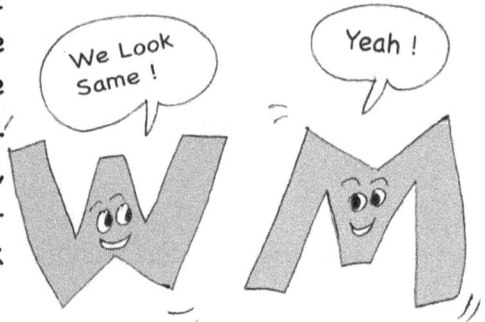

After that Jim said: I know the sound. It is Mm mm. Smart Jim!

WHAT A WAY TO DIVIDE THE STORY

The teacher had just finished reading a book.

Teacher: So what part of the story did you like?

Peter: The end of the middle of the story.

COOL SHIRT!

Brenden was wearing this shirt one day. It was pretty funny!

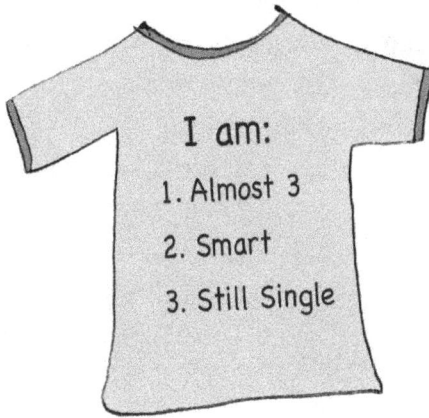

I am:
1. Almost 3
2. Smart
3. Still Single

KNOW YOUR MATH

Children were playing outside in the afternoon. Three of them were deciding about how they would be taking turns on the slide.

Sam (pointing at other kids): Okay, so you will go first, you second, and you third.

Brendan: It should be one, two and three. Sam, you need to learn your numbers.

TAKE IT EASY, BILLY

During our summer school program, we had a trip to the movies. That day we were going to watch 'HORTON HEARS A WHO'.

During one part in the movie, the elephant, Horton, was running for his life from his enemies. Billy and Max were sitting together and enjoying this scene. As soon as Billy saw this he started screaming: Oh no! The elephant is going to die.

Max: No, Billy. He is not going to.
Billy (almost in tears): Oh yeah, he is. Oh my God.
Max: Relax Billy, He is not going to die.
Billy (crying, sobbing): Uhh.....he is.
Max: Trust me Billy, he won't. I have seen this movie before.

That's my secret

School was almost over. Katie's mom came little early to pick her up. When she saw her mom she went running towards her.
Katie: Hi Mom.
Mom: Hey Katie, how are you? So what did you do today?
Katie: Nothing.
Mom: Well, you must have done some work, anything about Math, language, science?
Katie: Well, that's a surprise. I am not telling you.

A JOB FOREVER?

Molly's dad is in the Army. Molly and Emery were talking about it.

Molly: You know what, my dad is in the army. He fights against bad people.

Emery: Oh wow! So where is he now?

Molly: Today he is at home.

Emery: So is he fighting with the bad people in your neighborhood today?

I KNOW MORE THAN YOU

Emma and Emery were talking about goats, a very rare animal to talk about. But Emery seemed to have a lot of information.

Emma: Do you know where the baby goats come from?

Emery: Baby goat store.

Emma: Oh! I see.

WHO INVENTED BOOKS?

Now this is very common among the young boys, who are still learning to read.

Teacher: Hi Jack, let's read a book

Jack: No thanks, I am good.

PINK BELONGS TO THE GIRLS ONLY

Molly and Peter was coloring a grasshopper picture. After finishing their work, they both left their pictures on the teacher's desk. When the teacher came back, she saw no names were written on them and could not figure out whose work it was.

Teacher: Boys and girls, whose pictures are these?
Peter and Molly came forward.
Teacher (expecting the kids to write their names): How would I know which picture belongs to who?
Molly took her picture from the teacher. She picked a marker, did something on the picture and brought it back.
Molly: Here, the grasshopper with pink lipstick is mine.

I AM ON TEACHER'S SIDE

Sam and Peter were talking while the teacher was writing on the board. The teacher told them to listen what she was talking about.

Sam: You know teachers talk a lot all the time. They never let us talk.
Peter: Yeah. That is because they have a lot to tell us.

DON'T WE ALL MISS TV AT SCHOOL?

Matt was sitting on the table with his book open. Ms. Susan saw him not reading and came to him.

Ms. Susan: Hey Matt, I see that you are not reading your book.
Matt: Ms. Susan, I am sad.
Ms. Susan: Oh why? What happened?
Matt: When I stop working, I start thinking about TV.
Ms. Susan: What's the sad part?
Matt: I miss TV.

YOU ARE SO SWEET, PETER

The teacher had been talking about Migration since few days. When Brendan came to school that day, he was little sad. The teacher asked him about it.

Teacher: Oh Brendan, what happened?
Brendan: My mom's aunt died yesterday. She used to play with me.
Teacher: Oh I am so sorry.
Peter, who was listening, came over. He was really sympathetic.
Peter: Brendan, don't worry your aunt didn't die, she just migrated to Heaven.

THAT IS TRUE

The kindergartners were working with Ms. Kate about the countries, their capitals and flags.

Yes, I Know All !

Emery: Oh Ms. Kate, why do we have to write and do so much work about the countries. We can get all the information on Google. Right?

THAT'S 100% CORRECT

One morning Ms. Jen was counting the kids on the line.

Ms. Jen: So we have 11 boys and 7 girls. We have 2 girls missing today.

Molly: But also Ms. Susan is not in school either.

Peter: So that makes 3 girls missing.

Molly: No, that would be 2 girls and 1 lady missing.

MATH WIZARDS

Almost every day before lunch, a teacher would ask the kindergartners a question regarding math. One day I decided to trick them. And just as I thought they did start to count as soon the question was out.

Teacher: Yesterday I had a deer in my yard eating tulips. He ate 3 from the back yard, 2 from the front yard, 5 tulips near the garage and 4 near my car. (The kids are busy counting, counting, and counting. So engrossed, and hardly paying attention to what my question would be.)

Teacher: Okay, so the question is, Name the third planet from the Sun.

Kids (ALL TOGETHER): 14!

I CAN SCARE YOU TOO.

One of the older boys, Anthony had a fight with his best friend and was very upset. He was not working and was sitting on the table doing nothing. The teacher asked him several times to finish his work. After a while,

Teacher: You are not working and also not listening. Do you want me to tell your mom about it?
Anthony (still so mad): I have to call your mom too.
Teacher: Why?
Anthony (got scared for talking back): Not telling you.

YES, YOU ARE

Emery came back after a 7 day trip to Aruba. She was all tanned.
Teacher: Emery, you are all tan.
Emery: No, I am four.

OIL EXPLOSION

The teacher was talking about the Food Pyramid.

Teacher: Fruits and vegetables are good for you. You should eat them more. Do not eat oily things a lot.
Brendan: Yes, my mom said if we will eat too much oil, one day we can explode.

SMART ANSWER

Molly and Peter share their birthday on the same day. Sam did not know that. That day when it was their birthday, this was a cute little talk.

Molly: It's my birthday today.
Peter: Really! Mine too.
Sam: Are you twins?
Peter: Only if we were a family.

COME ON BILLY, IT'S NOT THAT HARD

The teacher was working with the kindergartners about the calendar.

Teacher: How many days are there in a year?
Billy: Its 300 and something.
Teacher: How many exactly?
Billy: I know its 300 and couple more.
Teacher: Come on, let's see. How many? How many?
Billy: I remembered last year was 365, but I don't know about this year.

REPETITION IS GOOD

The teacher was working with the kindergartners and writing about Birds on the chalkboard.

Teacher (while writing): They have a beak. They have feathers. They have claws.
Brendan: Why is the teacher writing 'They have' again and again?
Jack: Look at the good side. Now we will know how to write 'They have' forever.

NOW DO YOU GET IT?

Emery was working on her sentences. She was supposed to make a sentence with the word 'Cap'.

Emery: "The girl lost her cap".
Molly: What does lost mean?
Emery (angry): Lost means "loosed'. She looses it, means she couldn't find it. Now do you get it?

LONG, LONGER, LONGEST

Emma was reading a book to the teacher sitting right next to her.

Emma (reading): "While mom was cooking dinner, Jamie was watching TV." You know Ms. Jen, this is short for TV.

Ms. Jen: And what would be long for TV?

Emma: T.V. (T dot V dot)

Ms. Jen: Well, the full form for TV is Television.

Emma: Yeah, But that one is not long, that's the longest.

JUST MAKING SURE

Today the teacher was talking about mammals. She was writing about some animals that are mammals. Max had a question.

Max: What are Bats?

Teacher: They are mammals too.

Max: So they are just like us. Like a person.

Teacher: Yes.

Max (scared): So, so, so is it okay if they come close to you.

Teacher: Well.....

Max: Enhh....They won't bite us. Bats and I are mammals. Right, Teacher. (Still so scared)

LEAVE THEM ALONE, JACK

The kindergartners really work hard regarding the details about all the Presidents of USA in their binders. Jack was checking his work from the beginning, to see if did not miss any of them. While turning his written pages about the Presidents, I heard him say, dead...this one is dead .....this one too....dead.....dead.....still dead......one more......dead again......
And this went on for a while.

I am just smarter

Peter and Sam were talking during snack time about college stuff!

Peter: After 12th grade, you go to college when you are 18 years old.

Sam: No actually 12th grade is college and it doesn't matter, you can be 18 or 19 years.

Peter: How do you know, you are not even there yet.

Sam: How do you know? You are also not 18.

Peter: I just know things.

NO, NOT EVERYTHING

Peter and Anna were doing math work. They were supposed to write their numbers from 1 to 100. Looked like Peter had something else going in his mind. He started counting his numbers in the other way.

I will walk backwards today !

Peter: 10, 9, 8, 7, 6, 5........

Anna: Why are you counting backwards? Were you born backwards?

Peter: I am counting backwards but I was born forward, I think.

THE SHOW STOPPER

The dance teacher in our school had organized a big show with some kids in the theatre.
Next day in class,

Teacher: Max, I heard you were running and not dancing on the stage.
Max: I know (laughing).
Teacher: You were supposed to dance. So did you spoil the show?
Max: Yeah, I did. But my mom and dad were laughing and so was everybody else. I think it was funny. I did fantastic. That's what my mom said.

I AM JUST A KID, HOW WOULD I KNOW...

It was the gardening day. Teachers and kids were going to plant some flowers outside in the school yard.
Ms. Dana had dug some holes for the plants. Miles came to her to help.

Miles: Ms. Dana, what can I do?

Ms. Dana: Well, if you can take out some more dirt from this hole.

Miles (after watching it for a while): But there is no more dirt in the hole, it's empty.

WHITE BREAD MAKES YOU LOOK FAIR?

Molly has a very, very fair complexion. One day during lunch time,

Anna: Do you eat the bread with grains?
Molly: No, I can't. I am allergic to wheat. I only eat rice bread.
Anna: Oh! That's why you are so white.

NAUGHTY MOMMY

Teacher: Who is the naughtiest one in your house?
Brendan: My mom.
Teacher: Really! How is that?
Brendan: She stops me from standing on the chair, but then she stands on it to get something from the cabinet.

BUSY BEES

Jack and Peter had finished their math work. They wanted to do more but it was almost lunch time and the teacher had told them to put their work away.

Jack: My head is so boring.
Peter: What does that mean?
Jack: It means my head is bored.
I have nothing to do.
Peter: Oh! Mine too then.

LUCKY 5TH GRADERS

The teacher and Sarah were on the same table for lunch.

Teacher: So Sarah what grade is your brother Aidan in?
Sarah: He is in the grade where you can buy things.
(I asked her dad about it the next day. He said Aidan is in 5th grade and he gets some allowance to buy his own stuff).

IT IS A COLOR FOR ME

Three children were coloring flower pictures, on the art table.

Emery: Mine is a red flower.
Anna: Mine is a blue flower.
Emma: Mine is a beautiful flower.
Anna: What? That's not even a color.

LISTEN CAREFULLY

Sam and Billy, both kindergartners are talking about their future.

Sam: My mom said we have a lot of money for my college.
Billy: But you didn't even go to college. Okay tell me what do they do in 11th grade.
Sam: I think you didn't get what I just said. Did you?

THE CHICKEN IS ON VACATION

Brendan and Olivia were doing the chicken crossing the road questions.

Brendan: Why did the dinosaur cross the road?
Olivia: I don't know. But where is the chicken. Isn't he supposed to cross the road? Where did the dinosaur come from?

WAY TO GO

Now this conversation was very interesting. Sometimes you will notice how the children continue their conversation and how two dialogues are connected.

Debbie: Last night I went for trick or treat. I got about 30 candies.
Jack: Candies are very bad for our teeth.
Billy: Yeah, you can get cavities.
Jack: My grandpa has cavities.
Billy: My grandpa is in Heaven.
Debbie: Yeah, God is in Heaven and also in church.
Jack: I go to church every Sunday.
Billy: I go to play soccer every Sunday.
Debbie: My brother plays baseball.
Billy: My brother is 11 years old but he still didn't go to college.
Jack: My grandma is 85 and she still didn't die.
Debbie: My grandma lives in New York.
Jack: I never went to New York, but I did go to California.
Debbie: Yeah, Disney is in California.
Billy: But I watch Nickelodeon, not Disney.
Jack: I watch SpongeBob on Nick.
Debbie: I don't even like SpongeBob.
And I don't know when and how this longest conversation ever ended. From Halloween candies to SpongeBob? Oh Boy!

NOT FOR BOYS

Emma: Is this your lipstick, Marc?
Marc: It's lipstick for girls. For boys it's called Chap Stick.

ARE YOU SURE IT'S NOT CONSTELLATION....

Billy: My dad took me out last night on our drive way and showed me the 'Star constipation'.

TOUGH GALS

The children were playing outside. Brianna had been running for a long time. Sam was also playing with her, he saw her sweating. He came to her.

Sam: Hey Brianna, you are sweating.
Brianna: My Mom says girls don't sweat, they glow. So I am glowing!

LOVE AT FIRST SIGHT?

Peter, Miles and Molly were on the lunch table. While eating, Peter and Molly were looking at each other.

Peter: Wow! You have beautiful eyes.
Molly: Thanks.
Peter: When I grow up, I'll marry Molly.
Miles (jealously): But then you have to be older. You and Molly are both six, so you can't.

NOBODY CAN TRICK ME......I AM SMART

Max was painting with the water colors. He had paint on his hands, shirt and all over. I thought of tricking him. I said," Max, You have some paint on your nose". I thought he would touch his nose with his messy hands. Instead he looked at me and kept staring for a while. Then he said," I think you are tricking me." I asked him how he could figure that out.

> I am the smartest !

$$3n=4, n=?$$
Math $x+y+z=0$
$$E=mc^2$$
CH_3COOH
Science
$a+b-ab$

Max: My mom tricks me like that all the time. So I know all about these kind of tricks. I am very smart.

QUICK RESPONSE, ISN'T IT?

Marc and Billy were washing their hands in the bathroom. It was winter time.

Marc: Oooh! The water is so cold.
Billy: Whenever I wash my hands with cold water, it makes me go pee.

> Hurry up, I have to go too!

KIDS LOVE PATTERNS

Bob and Michael walked in together in the class that morning. They were both hanging their back packs in their cubbies. I heard this funny conversation from the other side (unknowingly, of course).

Bob: You know what, I took bath today.

Well, I save a lot on water, soap and shampoo !

Michael: I didn't. I bath on Sundays.

Bob: Every Sunday?

Michael: No, one Sunday I do, the next Sunday I don't, then again one Sunday I do, then don't. It's a pattern.

I LOVE YOU, BANANA

Max loves bananas. Ms. Dana was eating one for her lunch. Max, who was sitting next to her, was looking at her and he was licking his lips. It looked like he wished he had that banana. Ms. Dana kept on eating and she was all the way to half. Max could not wait any more.

Max: Ms. Dana, are you going to finish that whole banana?

I love you, banana !

HELLO JELL-O ...CAN I HAVE MORE

Most of the time, a birthday kid would bring a goody bag for each of the classmate. The teachers would put these goody bags in the student's go home folders. It was Anna's birthday. Her mom had brought some homemade Jell-O for snack. After the snack was over, there was a lot left. Billy wanted to have more. He went to the teacher.

Billy: Ms. Kate, could you put some left over Jell-O in my go home folder?

OH GOODNESS!

Brenden had been in the bathroom for a long time. The teacher knocked at the door and she asked if she could come in. Brenden opened the door and he had the toilet paper in his hand.

People distract me all the time !

Teacher: Brenden, you had been in the bathroom for a long time. Do you need help?
Brenden: I was cleaning the walls.
Teacher: Walls? Why?
Brenden: Well, I was standing and peeing and suddenly Jack opened the door and started talking to me, when I looked at him he made me pee everywhere. Even on the walls.

CAN'T WAIT

This is a very common answer from the girls each time you ask.

Teacher: What would you like to be when you grow up?

Girl: Mommy!

OOPS......

Jack: Yesterday I spilled milk on my mom's dress.

Teacher: Oops...Then what did you do?

Jack: Nothing. I blamed it on my sister.

Teacher: She didn't say that you were lying?

Jack: No. She is not even two, can't talk yet!

NEXT GENERATION, ALWAYS AHEAD.

Miles: I don't know why my dad is always cranky.

Max: I think all the dads are, because they have a lot of work to do. May be when you will grow, you will be cranky too.

Miles: Well my little baby brother is already very cranky. He is way ahead of his schedule, I guess.

TOO LATE, MISTER

Ms. Dana was wearing a beautiful shirt. She was looking very pretty. Jack and Molly came in and saw her sitting on the table reading to another child.

Jack (whispering): I love Ms. Dana. I am going to marry her.
Molly: But she is already married.
Jack: Oh no!

ALL GRANDPAS DO

During the line time, Emma kept on yawning. She looked very tired.

Teacher: Emma, you look very tired. Did you not sleep last night?
Emma: No, I slept with my grandparents and my grandpa snores very loud. I could hardly sleep.

ALWAYS WATCHING YOU

Jack and Peter were doing a puzzle work. Peter was looking for one particular piece. He couldn't find it.

Peter: Where is it? I wish I had more eyes.
Jack: My mom said she has 4 eyes. But I see only two.
Peter: I think she hides the other two eyes.

PLEASE TAKE CARE OF YOUR THINGS

Sam was doing his work on the rug. After some time he started looking around as if he had lost something. I went to him.

Teacher: Sam, are you looking for something?

Sam: Yeah, I had my booger on the finger.

Teacher: What about it?

Sam: Where is it now?

HOT LEMONADE

The teacher was laminating some papers in the teacher's room. Jackie came to her to show her finished work.

Jackie: What are you doing Ms. Kate?

Ms. Kate: I have to laminate these papers.

(Jackie stood there until Ms. Kate was done. She switched the laminator off. Jackie stood there still waiting for something).

Ms. Kate: Okay Jackie, let's go.

Jackie: But where is the lemonade. You said you were making lemonade.

Ms. Kate: Laminate Jackie, not lemonade.

MAY BE

Sarah was working on her writing work. She kept dropping her pencil on the floor.

Catch me if you can!

Teacher: Sarah, you have to hold your pencil tight while writing.
Sarah: Otherwise it will run away?

I AM BEING TRUTHFUL

Molly was coloring a picture of a girl. She colored the eyes red. Peter was sitting next to her. He was looking what Molly was doing.

Peter: Why are you coloring the eyes red?
Molly: Actually this is me and I am coloring the eyes red because I have allergies.

THESE KIDS KNOW EVERYTHING

One day it was raining very heavily. When it was recess time to go outside, the teacher told the children that they will not be able to play outside.

Marc: But why can't we go outside to play?
Teacher: Look how rainy it is outside. It's raining cats and dogs. (Next day again when it was almost time to go out again, it started raining. But this time it was very less. Just sprinkles.)
Brendan: Can we go out today? It's raining only kittens and puppies.

I DO KNOW THE MAGIC WORD

It was Jackie's birthday and she had brought fruits and muffins for snack as a treat. All the children were sitting for the snack to be served.

Ms. Dana: Peter, here is your fruit and muffin.
Peter: Thank you, Ms. Dana.
Ms. Dana: Here Molly, this is your share.
Molly: Thank You, Ms. Dana.
Ms. Dana: Sam, your fruit and muffin.
Sam: Thank You, Ms. Dana.
Ms. Dana: Brendan, this is for you.
(Brendan did not say anything. Ms. Dana stood there waiting for his thank you reply. Brendan was totally unaware why the teacher was looking at him.)
Ms. Dana: So Brendan, what is the magic word?
Brendan: Ehh……Abracadabra? Is it?

24 PLUS

Max: Yesterday was a long day. I think it was 28 hours long.

Emma: No, it is always 24 hours in a day.
Max: But I think it was longer, because when my dad came back from his work, he was telling my mom that it was a long day today.

ONE SUN IS ENOUGH TO MAKE IT HOT

It was a hot day. The children were curious to know if they would get the chance to play outside.

Max: My mom told me not to go outside today to play.

Anne: Why?

Max: Because it is going to be very, very hot.

Anne: Do you think there will be two Suns coming out today?

PARTY TIME, BATH TIME

Jack: My dad takes shower every day before he goes to work, so that he can feel fresh and clean.

Peter: Well, my dad takes bath only when he has to go to a party.

SIMPLEST RECIPE!

Sarah: I know how to make 'Sprite'.

Molly: Buy one bottle of Sprite from the store and keep it on your party table!

OH NO!

Peter: My mom can make Black forest cake.

Jack: How?

Peter: She just burns the regular cake in the oven!

UMMHH...

The teacher could smell something weird around in the classroom. She kept walking around and asking everyone if they could smell it too.

Marc: It does smell little. Did you take bath today, Jack?

Jack: Wait a minute, one day 'yes', one day 'no' and then one day 'yes'.

Marc: So which one is today?

Jack: I think it is one day 'no'.

SWEET DREAMS

Ms. Dana was talking about Martin Luther King, a week before MLK day.

Ms. Dana: So as I told you about Dr. King's speech, "I have a dream", I would like all of you to write about your dream too.

Brendan: But Ms. Dana, I don't even see dreams. I only have nightmares.

MOMMY WAS HUNGRY?

Marc and Bobby were talking about their birthdays.

Marc: Bobby, how were you born?
Bobby: I don't know. My mom told me that I was in her tummy.
Marc: In her tummy? Why did she even eat you in the first place?

MOST IMPORTANT

Brenden: Ms. Jen, I know the secret ingredient for the cookies.
Ms. Jen: What is it, Brenden?
Brenden: 'Sugar'!

YEAH, THAT'S WHAT WE ALL CALL I˙

Jack: I call lunch and dinner time, "Stuff my belly time."

THE END

Ms. Jen was writing few sentences on the board. She was working with the kindergartners.

Ms. Jen: Okay, let us finish it up with this last sentence. Tortoise and turtles are reptiles
Anna: Ms. Jen, you forgot to put the pyramid at the end.
Ms. Jen: Pyramid? Do you mean a period?
Anna: Yeah, period. This is so confusing.